Conversations with Ali:

Reflections of a Soldier

*Jamie,
If we never meet again, Have a beautiful life.*

For Corporal Michael E. Thompson

KIA Sept 18 2008

Operation Iraqi Freedom

"Though he should conquer a thousand men in the battlefield a thousand times, yet he, indeed who would conquer himself is the noblest victor."

-Buddha

"Blessed are the peacemakers, for they will be called sons of God".

-Jesus

Preface

Death was a part of my life and has shaped it from a very early age. When I was a child I learned my mother died while staying with my grandmother in Virginia. She was a good woman, who I did not treat well enough. My mother is a woman I can barely remember, and is therefore an idealized figure. I lost a guide and a friend when I lost my mother. Although I wouldn't know it for many years later. At the funeral we were asked to touch the casket several times and pray. People need rituals. It was a visceral experience for me, a child of eight years. I remember she had "ticklers". Her hands that were often covered in IVs at the hospital. It was from the way my father cared for her though twenty years of sickness that taught me to be a man. We can never live up to the examples of our fathers, if we had good ones that is. I remember used to sing, Silver and gold might buy You a home. But things of this world, they won't last you long".

I remember a girl I loved very much. It was a young love, and pure love. It burned brightly, and fizzled out. I remember standing in the snow having just been handed a break up note. The solitary darkness of the night has never grown in upon me at any time in my life than in that moment. I remember the child we were going to have, the reason I joined the Army. The reason I went on this journey at all. I would try to be a man and support my family, just as my father had, as I stood in the snow that night I remember very little of what I did next. Inside the note which was neatly folded, a diamond ring I bought at an Army base in Maryland. It has been fourteen years. I still have the ring. While I have moved on with my life and live with a person I love just as much. I remember that girl and I love her. I remember "Talvari". It's as clear to me as Mount Rainier on a clear day. I can hear it like the music of the forest birds. They should have sent a poet to write this story. I feel it is worth telling because it is so middle of the road shall we say. It is average, normal, and mundane, filled with the stabs of pain and the shrieks of fear we all experience from one day to the next. Can a sad man write a happy book? Can a happy man write a sad book? Can I write a book at all? My dear Theopolis I have been both these things, and asked all three questions. Perhaps the most important question I ask about this work is if it is worthy of being written or read at all? Humility in all things, respect in all things. Remember all of us must die. I wait for it. You have found out a bit why in the preceding introduction. We shall find out why I am still waiting. Should you discover this text and I am dead go sit under a tree in the warm summer air and enjoy the beauty of the day. I hope I lived a long life full of more joy than pain. More love than hatred, and more than being remembered for anything great, I hope I lived my life respected and died regretted. One thing I know for certain. I am not, nor have I ever been a hero.

Joseph Soel,

Olympia WA

December 24th 2019

Nestled in the Hills of Bristol the Wooded Shore

Chapter One

My name is Joe. Even as I sit in this smoke-filled bar, the crackling of pool balls behind me filling the air as well, my name feels unimportant. I could be any veteran, and man who ventured out and tried at his nation's behest to do his duty. I could have been any man that came back and felt embittered and lost, sent off to fight a war the value of which I am unsure. I went for my comrades, and was prepared to die for those next to me should the situation arise. Thankfully it did not. This willingness to die, and this acceptance of death were due to the love of my comrades. The foolishness of youth the same the world over. Many millions of boys have put on uniforms and have. Marched off, and all of them assume they are invincible. Have we learned anything from our past? Perhaps not.

The TV news is on, and ISIS is on the rise in Iraq. Maybe we shall have another war over there whether we want it or not.

My path to Iraq began on September 11th, 2001. I was sitting in Mrs. Jacob's freshman world history class; I don't remember what we were learning about. A knock came at the door, and our teacher was called outside. She appeared about 30 seconds later, crying, and shaking. The TVs were down due to a recent fire on campus a few days prior. Someone turned on a radio, and we heard the bulletin. Two planes had struck the World Trade Center in New York City, and there were reports of an explosion at the Pentagon in Virginia. There was also an unknown number of possible hijacked aircraft in the air. My blood ran cold. I knew then at 14 years old, my future lay in military service. The attacks that shaped my generation, and our culture for better and worse, the twenty years since that event, were propelling me headfirst into my own small date with history. We would be going to war, I wanted to help avenge those who had been killed. I knew I wanted to do something to help respond to the attacks.

In the coming days, President Bush reassured the nation that we would hunt down and punish those responsible for the attacks in New York, Washington, and Pennsylvania. Being a New Yorker myself, I hoped he was damned right. I was overflowing with a patriotic spirit and a bloodlust for vengeance. So many others were as well.. The National Guard was deployed to airports. All flights were shut down, and in New York City, and the scene was one of a war zone, with rubble, fires, and body parts were strewn about Manhattan. Calls for revenge were coming from both parties, and President Bush's approval rating was in the range of the 90th percentile. This environment of anger, and calls for war was enough to warp the minds of a generation. Not that the rage was not justified. Our pastor talked about righteous indignation. But it took us down the path to a war that had nothing to do with 9/11 itself. This would be a war that would cost the lives of 4,486 American soldiers, and an unknown number of Iraqis, combatants and noncombatants alike.

One must wonder how we got there as a people, the invasion, the occupation, the torture at Abu Ghraib. Stains upon the very fabric that is the American flag that was stained red with the blood of honorable American Soldiers. Soldiers who were willing to die. To strike back for the attacks upon the very heart of our nation. We have seen the Patriot Act violate our civil liberties. We have been witnesses to the invasions of the countries of Afghanistan, Iraq, and interventions in Libya, and Syria. When we look back upon the last years, I used to put a number on them, but they just keep going on. Since the attacks, it is a miracle the situation did not get worse for us.

The fact that they did not speaks volumes about the strength of our institutions. People in other nations have suffered greatly. An international perspective shows that the hate expressed on 9/11 now permeates the lives of many millions of people the world over. I became an ordained minister and a Buddhist because of my experiences during this time. I have spent my life since the war seeking spiritual truth and peace. We need to care for our fellow human beings if we want to overcome the pain of this period in our history. I'm sorry to say, but the last 20 years have been a dark time for our Country and the world at large. This is not to place blame on one person or another. But If we believe that killing and causing suffering is wrong, then we must take steps to prevent wars in the future.

It was 2003, and I was in a high school business class. The teacher, whose name I have lost to time, had written the words, Operation Iraqi Freedom, on the board. On 9/11 and in the days after, we had talked with our teachers as a class. We had asked fearful questions. Are we going to war? How long will the war last? Will there be other attacks? Worry and fear were paramount in those days. I had no way of knowing how caught up in this national march toward revenge I would become.

My story of war is not one of valor. I am genuinely by no means a hero. I did not serve in the infantry or in a "front-line" unit, and I was too young to participate in the initial invasion of Iraq. Still, I joined the Army anyway in April of 2006. This decision would shape the rest of my life and take me across the North American continent, to Europe, and the Middle East. It was the Middle Eastern part of my wanderings that would be the most formative of my entire life. I am still figuring out what to make of them. Most of the trips to various bases around the continental United States were in preparation for my deployment to Iraq. What the deployment did to me is hard to put into words. This book is, in a way, an attempt at healing for me. The gut-wrenching poverty, the fear of mortar attacks, the fear of the Iraqis themselves, was enough to change my option of geopolitical affairs, as well as concepts of human morality.

Here I must add a personal note for those in my unit, who may recognize the stories in this humble accounting of our time together. I love you. You were, and are my brothers and sisters. Your service was honorable because you knew our cause to be just. You are now, and were then, fathers, sons, daughters, husbands, and wives. I wish to take nothing from you by submitting my account. I remember it as, perhaps not merely in fact but in feeling. Should you find an issue with what I have written, only know that I have no question that you are men and women of the utmost integrity and honor. I was and am a better person for having known you.

No, my story is not one of glorious combat or heroic deeds. I am more Billy Pilgrim than Achilles. Of valorous acts, I fear I am in very short supply. My story is simply of a man, making his way in the world and had I been a monk instead of a soldier, my pleas for peace would not seem so strange. But because I was a soldier, I must call for peace. Not because wars in their causes are inherently wrong, or because warriors do not have a shred of indignity in them, but because I must. If I do not call for peace, how I shall justify my contribution to the suffering of others. Even in a small and ancillary way, it is absolutely nothing but an unclosed wound upon my soul. In the invasion of Iraq and occupation of Iraq I can find no *Casus belli*. However soldiers do not get to decide where we are sent. These questions are for us to sort out later. Everyone must come to their own conclusions about their wartime service. For me it is pride in doing my duty, and sadness for causing suffering.

    I have as it were, unfinished business, that I shall not allow another to finish it for me. I have guilt and pain, pride, and some shame. Mostly I have grief. Grief and sadness for the families of those lost, maimed, and those discarded, and those left behind. Still waiting for relief in line at the VA or suffering on the streets. For those 22 veterans a day who take their own lives. I have to write this down to get it out of me, shed it from myself. And let it be a humble offering upon the shrine of those lost. May God forgive me, and may we all be able to forgive ourselves.

I think only in my judgment of the actions of our government judgments upon the system which has predicated them. I do not judge you, my friends. This is my conviction, my sentence, as one imposed upon myself, and not upon those of you, I called brother and sister. To my fellow soldiers, I would say that we were victims of the war, as much as the civilians who lived in the war zone were. My personal experience with war does not preclude my responsibility to rebalance my karma, however. Others can deal with whatever guilt they feel in their own way, even not at all, but I must remove this from myself.

We, as a nation, must admit and confront the Islamophobia that is rampant in our country. We can see clear evidence of it in the military. In training, that was used to indoctrinate soldiers to go off for the war in Iraq and Afghanistan. We were taught to call the locals *Hajjis*. The more you used degrading language in basic training, in regards to the enemy, the more we were praised. I remember being praised for yelling "Die Hajji, Mother Fucker", on the bayonet course, while stabbing a dummy with a rag on its head. Dehumanization of the enemy is a huge problem, as it allows for those who want war to convince human beings to engage in war. The leaders and their children seldom seem to be the ones risking their lives.

What it all comes down to is what kind of world we want to live in. We must put all nationalist fervor aside when considering this question. What kind of world do we want? Those who wish to live in a peaceful world must rise and fight peacefully, and heartily for it. Violence is a horrible thing that we visit upon our fellows. Every human being has value. I must stand for, a better world. But that does not make me a better person. I want a world that takes care of everyone instead of justifying violence upon one another because we are different from them culturally, religiously.

If my service in Iraq has taught me anything, it is that we are not different from the Iraqi people in any way that matters. We see the presumptive Republican presidential nominee calling for a total and complete shutdown of all Muslims entering the country. The people I knew in Iraq were good. I cannot believe he is doing anything but pandering to people's fear, but it is disturbing nonetheless.

We must stand for peace and justice. Our country, The United States of America, has to stop being an empire at some point.

How much longer can we police the entire world? As we see from the lesson of Rome and the dissolution of colonial empires after World War Two, the party does not last forever. We can either suffer through the eventual decline, or we can build a better world for all people. War and killing are never in the interest of ordinary people. We must decide. If we look truly into our hearts I think very few of us would want war. Peace is always better for everyone. Peace allows for creation and stability. I believe war should be avoided at all costs. It should be a last resort, not a status quo.

To Kill Without Mercy: A Soldier's Education

Chapter Two

Drill Sergeant Sides is a man not to be fucked with.

He was in the 3rd Armored Cavalry.

He tells us stories of when he was at Fort Knox as a "baby Cav Scout."

He teaches us to "learn from it and drive on".

A lesson I will rely upon in my darkest times.

He screams in our faces, the most heinous insults.

We love him for it.

He tortures us while he teaches us.

He teaches as he tortures.

He's seen his share of action and tells us we will see the same.

He's preparing us not to die, that's his "Mother Fucking Job."

He can teach us to deal out death, but not to deal with death.

As far as I know, we didn't lose anyone from our class in Iraq

Sometimes I look when I've been drinking.

Learn from it and Drive the fuck on!

"Drill Sergeants are the cautioning voice, the helpful hand, the watchful eye that guides the new soldier through strenuous Army Training.

They have gained their knowledge through practical experience. It is appropriately their job to guide, instruct, and encourage young people who are training to become soldiers."

Actual quotes from my Drill Sergeants. (This is all a mind fuck)

"Drill Sergeants are here to fuck up your day, son. Don't thank me, thank your recruiter. Jodie is fucking your girl right now. You should have been the load your momma swallowed. The best part of you ran out of your mommas pussy and down her ass crack.

You better not drop that fucking hand grenade. SHOW ME YOUR FUCKING WAR FACE PRIVATE!!"

We love and hate them. We miss the "Drills," and we never want to see them again. I saw one in Kuwait once, I walked right by. I didn't say a fucking word.

For a lot of reasons, patriotism and nationalist fervor aside, I was a victim of what some call the "poverty draft." I say I got a girl pregnant when we were 18 and had no money. "Potato Pa-"you done fucked up kid". I am from the northeast, and thanks to the NAFTA treaty, the heavy industry had taken a hit. Long before the crash of the global economy in 2008 there was no real stable work to speak of. When all was said and done, there was very little for a High School graduate to do in Honeoye, New York. My hometown of about 600 residents had several shuttered factories. So in place of moving to the city in search of my fortune, I opted for a bigger adventure. I chose the Army Reserves, mostly because my recruiter told me I would probably be spending a significant amount of time on active duty anyway. With that and some wrangling with shady recruiting methods, I care not to mention that I went to MEPS (Military Entrance Processing Station). In Syracuse, NY. My fellows and I all underwent a gauntlet of physical exams, checking for spine disorders, and performing a duck walk in our underwear with doctors looking on. Some men were weeded out by the doctors, which always shattered them. Those who passed the medical exam, the academic testing and background checks were ushered in to sign their contracts.

The government must take a lesson from the tobacco companies because ninety-five percent of the enlistees seemed 18-22 years of age. Hook them while they're young, as it were. Among the papers that I signed, which felt like one hundred in total, was a declaration that I was not a homosexual. Nor bisexual, and that later admission to the contrary would be considered a breach of contract. While that was not expressly true, I signed anyway. "Don't Ask, Don't Tell" was still in full effect. As a picture of President Bush looked down upon me from the office wall behind the civilian, I was working with, I signed on the dotted line. After some time we were ushered into a room, where we all raised our right hands and took the oath of enlistment.

"I, _____, do solemnly swear that I will support and defend the Constitution of the United States against all enemies, foreign and domestic; that I will bear true faith and allegiance to the same; and that I will obey the orders of the President of the United States and the orders of the officers appointed over me, according to regulations and the Uniform Code of Military Justice. So help me, God."

With that, I was honor-bound to deploy wherever and whenever I was ordered to. We were shuttled to the airport in a van of some kind and thus began my travels. I remember very little about the flight to Louisville, KY. Other than takeoff, and looking at how small everything looked! It was my first time flying. I remember arriving at the USO in the Louisville airport, talking with the other enlistees, and boarding the bus to Fork Knox, but these are fragmented memories. Sometimes, time in the Army feels like one big long day, at least it did to me anyway. I recall a drill sergeant screaming "get the fuck off my bus", in the early hours of the morning. Filling out paperwork, and being issued "Marshmallows," army sweatpants and a sweatshirt, so-called because they make you look like a walking marshmallow. I remember being told that we only had a few hours to sleep, so get some rest for the big day tomorrow. I barely slept an hour.

Reception Battalion, at Fort Knox, was pretty straight forward. It was disheartening to be far away from home, for a kid barely a year out of high school.

I don't think that I made the adjustment very well. Well enough to squeeze by in any event, however. More medical and dental exams were to follow. Eye exams, blood tests, and oh the shots. We were lined up and walked through a row of nurses with needles, one after the other, and one TB test shot in each of our forearms. The transfer to the Basic Training Companies would come soon. We were, most of us, scared and excited, and terrified. Would all the horror stories be true? We were about to find out. Some would thrive in a stress-filled environment; others would crumble. We were taught, sometimes overtly, to view those who could not cut it with contempt. But looking back upon it now with a decade of perspective, it mattered little, those that washed out may have been better off; in fact, it may have saved their lives and their sanity. It was at Fort Knox Kentucky I learned that my girlfriend had lost the baby.

According to the Army, basic training is, "Designed to produce new soldiers who are motivated, disciplined, physically conditioned, trained in the common soldierly skills, and capable of taking their place in the ranks of the army in the field." [i]

Basic training is also designed to make Killers. Killing is reinforced. Over and over again to the point where it becomes an accepted part of every activity, like going lunch. When called to the attention, you will respond by screaming KILL! At the top of your lungs. Now, how many times where we called to attention? Too many to remember Kill became like hello, or goodbye. One vivid day that stuck with me from that early time was the bayonet training. Standing in a covered, open-air sandpit wearing full combat gear, we fix bayonets and spread apart at intervals as to not stab each other. Over a loudspeaker, a drill sergeant bellows, what is the purpose of the bayonet? "To kill to kill to kill without mercy, to kill to kill to kill without regret"! We are told to shout back. "What makes the green grass grow"? "Blood blood. Bright red blood"! Other generic chants include "Kill the women, Kill the children!" The running bayonet range would later test our proficiency, as we ran through, and stabbed and beat our targets, yelling kill KILL KILL, I ran upon one of the targets. I yelled, "DIE HAJJI MOTHER, FUCKER!" Disturbingly I was praised for this, as it showed the "right motivation" and "violence of action". Genuine hatred for the enemy. Every soldier, regardless of MOS (Military occupational specialty), goes through basic training in an "infantry Battalion. At least I did with Bravo Company 1/46 INF. In the end, we are all expendable cannon fodder, if need be, and the situation is desperate enough. You fight if you have to.

The cadences in boot camp also reinforced killing as a natural activity. Something that was not only normal but should be respected and praised.

"I went to the local market, where all the women shot, I pulled out my machete and then began to chop, Left right left right left right KILL! Left right left right you know I will"

"I went to the local playground where all the children play, I took out my Uzi, and I began to spray. Left-right, left-right, Left Right KILL!"

One cadence I recall even worked in the statement, "I want to drink Iraqi Blood." As we turn a cold analytical eye on this, we can see that one cannot send troops to occupy foreign lands without establishing separation with the enemy. One should not be a "Hajji Lover." I would later be called that in Iraq, by some of the jokers. While it was merely in jest it shows an undercurrent of dehumanization. Oddly enough by 2008 we are also supposed to be "winning hearts and minds". Soldiers, while deployed, will often destroy each other with cut downs. But it's all in god natured jest. You fuck with people. People fuck with you. It passes the time. One must develop a thick skin if one wants to survive. Nine weeks of this intense physical and psychological training, and one could mold a soldier.

Not everyone made it through. Some were too weak, others unmotivated, or had lost heart; one or two were simply not smart enough but had been pushed through MEPS. The war in Iraq was in full swing in 2006, and the Army needed all the warm bodies it could get. Deployments had to be filled, stateside positions filled, and the war had to continue. It is, of course, interesting to note that while the Army takes heat for how they choose to prosecute a fight, it is never the Army that starts the battle. It is always a politician.

It's always men who "had better things to do" when they were called to military service who start the next war. They got deferments during Vietnam, but would ask another generation of poor Americans to go die in their place, to protect their sorry hides, and enrich themselves in the process. All a politician or businessman can do in that situation is to make a profit off the suffering of other human beings. When you remove all the other platitudes, niceties, and just simply bullshit, it comes down to money. Plain and simple. Clear as day. Does that make the loss of a soldier dishonorable, or stain his service? Of course not. It stains the politician or the businessman. Nothing can stain the honor of a soldier who is ready to die for his friends.

As I attempt to think back upon boot camp, the gas chamber stands out to me. We marched there. I remember that. I'm not sure how far it was, but it was long enough to make you suffer. Herded like cattle, we were lined up again, because hey it's the Army, and walked into a concrete box. Once inside, we were ordered to remove our mask and recite the soldier's creed.

The Soldiers Creed
"I am an American Soldier.
I am a Warrior and a member of a team.
I serve the people of the United States and live the Army Values.
I will always place the mission first.
I will never accept defeat.
I will never quit.
I will never leave a fallen comrade.
I am disciplined, physically, and mentally tough, trained, and proficient in my warrior tasks and drills.
I always maintain my arms, my equipment, and myself.
I am an expert, and I am a professional.
I stand ready to deploy, engage, and destroy the enemies of the United States of America in close combat.
I am a guardian of freedom and the American way of life.
I am an American Soldier."

By the time "I am" left my lips, my lungs were on fire. Coughing, snorting and just dripping with sweat. We had to remain in the chamber until we had finished, we'll go with reciting for lack of a better term, the creed. Really, we coughed it out, unable to take a breath. We piled out snot dripping from our mouths, noses, and eyes. One way to clean yourself out from seasonal allergies, but not my first choice. The gas chamber is designed to show you the seriousness of warfare with biological and chemical weapons. It is designed to train you that if you do not put on your masks as fast as fucking possible or you will be fucking dead. What sort of serious business had I gotten myself into? I missed home!

    The relationship a soldier has with his rifle in boot camp or in a war zone is likely to be the most intimate one you will have while there. You eat with your rifle, sleep with your rile. Your rifle is everything to you, and respect for it is taught. You know every inch of her. How to strip her down to her barest components, and put her back together. You know how to lube her up. You know how to treat her right. One does not take the rifle lightly. The rifle is holy to the soldier. I remember feeling such pride when drawing my first rifle from the armory. It felt good in my hands, and it went everywhere with me for nine weeks. On deployment, the rifle would you go with me longer. Sometimes I am not sure I ever put it down. I turned it in,

I took off my uniform and went to college. I still miss that rifle. Number 7174653.

The military is what sociologists call a total institution, like a prison, or a monastery. It did feel like a mixture of both. There was a lot of stress, you were exhausted most of the time, sweaty and tired. You were lonely, and you could not leave. It also had a holy feel to it. Continually reinforced was that we were better than our peers in civilian society because we had signed up to serve the war effort. It took on an almost religious significance, as the Army's values became our own. One wanted to be honorable or to feel honored. You felt like you were a part of something greater than yourself, which is why so many veterans feel isolated when they return home, they are warriors without purpose. Once a war is over, or the warrior is sent back to the world, he often feels like there is little he can do. He feels lost and unsure of what to do.

That transition for me would come later. After the war and the Army, there was a long, hard period of self-abuse. Self-medication the VA calls it. At the time, I called it getting fucked up. There were five long island iced teas a night. Seven to ten beers. I would wake up puking every morning, after a night of binge drinking, and then go right back out to do it again. With thirty thousand dollars in the bank at 21, what else was I to do? Give a fool a fortune, and watch him squander it. The drinking never really went away, my liver got too old for it to be that extreme. Or so I told myself. I could have four beers and be done with it for the evening, but according to the VA, that is still alcoholism. They may be right. I could see the title of "alcoholic" applied to me. I've even come to accept it, went to a few A.A meetings. I just wasn't ready. With six months sober now, I can say that I was for sure.

  Basic training graduation came slowly and painfully. Some did not make it at all. One kid Private Brock, cracked under pressure, and was recycled. We saw him getting fucked with, back in "red phase" the hardest, beginning phase of the training when our platoon was on to "blue phase". We had the mentality of prisoners, and the courage of the guards, Boot camp was like voluntary prison.

  Another man, Private John Love decided he had had enough and claimed he was a homosexual to get out. It worked for him, and he was sent home to Texas. Some people simply could not handle the pressure, or it simply was not for them. Either way, those men may have been better off than we, the "strong "who finished the road. We looked down on them when they left. The drill sergeants walked them out of the barracks, and as we stood on the line, everyone did an about-face, we literally turned our backs on the weak. We had no less contempt for them than the dirt under our combat boots. I no longer feel that way about them. Everyone has their own journey, but I am glad I made it through.

    The war was coming for us, and we all knew it. Our drill Sergeants had both served in Iraq and one had lost a finger. Looking at his hand, we knew we were in for it. Every one of us knew the call might be coming. Some of us made makeshift calendars to count the days, some wrote letters home, and some tried to be strong. We were boys working so hard to be men. We there to please our fathers. To advance ourselves, we had chosen a path of violence and service that would end either in our deaths, or in our destruction. War comes in many forms. There is a war before you are deployed. There is also the war after you come home. Fear and longing is mixed with determination, and sadness. Every soldier is afraid. Any man who says he is not is posturing. Before the war, I had believed in nationalism. I had believed in our President, our mission, and our flag. I still love my Country, and our flag but the blind following of any banner can lead to disaster for the followers and those in their path or rage. The individual must try to keep their counsel. After the 9/11 attacks, all we had was a rage. As one cadence put it. "We wanted to drink Iraqi blood".

Boot camp breaks you down as a civilian and builds you into what the Army wants you to be. It has to for you to function correctly on the battlefield, or in a combat zone. The institutions we allow for manipulating us never ceases to amaze me.
Drill Sergeant Henning had lost his finger in Iraq.
I seem to remember some story about RPG shrapnel or something. That finger or lack thereof really had to make you admire the man. Even when he was 'Smoking you until you fucking die".

Hajji Don't Surf Son
Chapter Three

The orders came like the dawn reaching her rosy red fingers over the hills in my home village. I had known it was coming for a while, but sitting there and waiting for it had been maddening. When the orders finally came, I was overcome by numbness, I would finally validate myself through deployment. I would honor my father, who had fought in Vietnam, and I would contribute to the vengeance for the 9/11 attacks. Vengeance reaps revenge, and war, more war, but I knew nothing of that then. Pride and fear, anticipation, and terror overcame me all at once, and I knew then that my life's trajectory had just changed. I had been attending community college only a few weeks ago, now I was off to active duty and merely had to get by on my part-time job until them. Would this be a chance to break with the monotony and frankly, crushing poverty of working a dead-end job? There would be many more dead-end jobs to come, but again I did not know that yet. All I knew was I was embarking upon a great adventure, the likes of which I had never dreamed. I learned many things on this quest. For what I questing for I was not sure. It was simply the restlessness of youth. Orders were to be followed, however. Fort Sill awaited me.

The desert has no enemies. It simply is. Searing heat and burning sands seep into everything unwise enough to enter it. The heat can make you dizzy, and cloud your mind with the mirage. When we landed in the Kuwaiti desert in 2008, and after shuttling in the middle of the night through the streets if Kuwait city, we reached Camp Buehring at Udairi, Kuwait named after Lieutenant Colonel Charles H Buehring who was killed in Bagdad on October 26, 2003. Even here in the safety of a large military camp, with quite frankly, many of the comforts of home. The heat baked us, even in our tents. This was to be our acclimation time. To get used to being in the desert before our trip north into the war zone. I drank so much water, I barely made it to the proto-john. We would spend our time there practicing convoy ops, just as we had at fort Sill, in what seemed like long ago, and in California before that. COB Adder was in our future, only one hundred or so clicks up the road.

  God forgives, the desert does not. Like all domains of nature, unprepared and unprotected, it will overtake you for the slightest affront to its dominion. We were young and arrogant, rich with pride, and weighed down by fear and apprehension. We had ten years of propaganda to help with our self-assured confidence. We were striking back for those lost in New York City, the attacks had taken care of our self-assured pride. We were fearful of course because, well, let's be honest, we had all seen the news. Iraq was a cauldron of violence and instability, and we were going into it. We must have been young, or young or crazy, or both all at once.

  We were in munitions. Dealers in death, for lack of a better analogy, as the man of peace I have become, I look back on my friends with love and pride, and I look back upon the work I took part in with discomfort. I can feel Iraq weighing upon my Karma. But if you want to get technical, we were in the service department of death. Fobbits are what the infantry troops called us anyway. We would most likely never leave the safety of the base. Our bombs would strike out, dealing death to our enemies, and those caught in between. Bombs don't care if you are the target, you know. They don't care if you are rich or poor, Iraqi or American. So we as Fobbits would not have to face a violent death in combat to do our duty. We would remain for most of our tour in the protective embrace of the barbed wire. But as we found out, death could still reach in. It could strike from above with little to no warning. A mortar strike had for the soldiers at COB Adder just before we arrived. The troops who had been there had told the story. Soldiers tell stories, all of them do, waiting around for one task or another.

I have taken into myself the Buddhist Idea that we must have compassion for all living beings. As the *Buddhist Bible* compiled by Dwight Goddard says about the realization of the eightfold path. ***"Having left the world, he fulfills the rules of the monks. He avoids the killing of living beings and abstains from it. Without stick of Sword, conscientious, full of sympathy and compassion, he is anxious for the welfare of all living beings."***[ii]

If we wish to have compassion for all living beings, we must avoid war and oppose it at every turn. I cannot say that I have become a complete pacifist, but I am as close to it as you can get, without denying my self-protection. Wars kill people, and that is the truth of them. No matter how noble war is believed or claimed to be, I think it is evil in them. We cannot exercise it by our ignorance, or by our glorification of it. I wonder about my complicity in the deaths of many. That is my burden to carry. No one else can carry it for me.

Of the mortars, I lived in constant fear, which would be just my fucking luck, caught by a 155, or a rocket fired from the back of a pickup truck, or from a tube time delayed by dry ice, to foul up a quick reaction force from the base. It was a rocket that gave me my first big scare. At least I think that's what I remember people saying in could have been a mortar as well. We had only been in the country a few days, to a week, and I was standing outside a neighbor's CHU, or containerized housing unit, talking about everything and nothing. Off in the distance, 155 illumination rounds lit up the sky. We were shooting something.

    As the big guns fired, the ground seemed to shake with terror. Being new to a war zone, I jumped with every bang and quake. "That's outgoing," the sergeant I was speaking with would say, taking drags off his cigarette. As we talked in the dark, the cherry lit up his face, the face of a hake, Drag, "that's outgoing, you nervous kid?"

Just then, the most fearful sound I ever heard pierced the night. Beautiful and terrible, its blades screamed in the night. Swooshing through the air, coming to give us a welcome to Iraq kiss. Screeching like a demon from the depths of hell, it met its mark, if it had one. Insurgents sometimes just fired blind. The rocket slammed into the ground with a sound like a train hitting a fireworks factory. I hit the ground hard as we had been taught to do in basic. Laugh, drag.

"That's incoming," the sergeant said. He looked down at me from his perch on the step, and said, still laughing, "Welcome to Iraq."

That's when the yelling started. "Incoming, Incoming Incoming!" The confusion, and the sirens, the giant voice, the mass communication system of the base shouted! "Attention COB Adder, we have received indirect fire. All non-essential personnel are to remain indoors, the current alert level is an alert level three. That is all."

As we all crammed into the bunker, nothing but a hollow concrete slab in a U shape with sandbags over it, that would not seem to be able to survive a direct hit, we found out some soldiers we unaccounted for. They had gone to a hookah lounge that the locals had set up nearby we found out later. The first Sargent was running around, with the smell of smoke in the air calling for combat lifesavers, as the rocket had sounded pretty close. Thankfully no one was wounded, no one was killed, and we found our missing troops. We all went to bed that night. I was a bit shaken, the others we perhaps the same. The first week on the job. Twelve months three weeks to go. Another mortar attack wounded a Romanian soldier at a small sub-camp down the road from us. They went out looking for revenge as I remember. There were more mortar attacks than I can remember. A few I still have dreams about.

The Ninety-Nine Beautiful Names of God

asmāʾu llāhi l-ḥusnāe

Chapter Four

This is Iraq as I experienced it. What I say in this work can be said to be the truth as I see it. I send my deepest love for all those in my unit, even those who may disagree with me. It was an honor to serve with you. I would not be who I am today without experiencing this journey with you.

The road was hot, and you could see waves of heat swirling off the asphalt in the distance. Sergeant Duval, Private First-Class Lincoln, and I were on the road again, under arches that were a relic from when Saddam's forces still controlled this Air Base. On our right were old dilapidated buildings that I always thought of as old Iraqi Barracks. But given their condition they could have predated the base by a long time. Going around the curve to our left was the ancient city of Ur of the Chaldeans. Its ghosts watched us as we passed; sizing up the trespassers, testing their commitment to this now harsh land that had been a paradise so long ago.

  Mesopotamia had been the cradle of civilization, the start of mankind's journey to organized society and, for all the worse, warfare. The great Ziggurat was visible from every part of the base, and it never ceased to take my breath away. The original had predated the Pyramid at Giza, by millennia, and now I lived in its shadow. What a strange journey for a kid from a small farming village in Upstate New York. I was there in the presence of history, but at the time, all I could think of was the damn heat. Godforsaken fucking heat. 120 degrees, like living in a hairdryer. Why had someone built an entire country inside of a hairdryer?

Our mission that day, and many other days like it, was to pick up some "local nationals", as the Army called them, and bring them to a worksite for expanding our ammunition supply point. To do this work, men from the village, and the larger city of Nasiriya, about 25 clicks away, flocked to the base to get a spot. They were hired by the Iraqi contractor, how subcontracted for KBR-Halliburton, or for the Army. We had brought American capitalism to the locals, all right. I never knew how much they got paid, but if my experience in manual labor was any indication, comparatively speaking, it was not much. I didn't realize at my first visit to the Visitor Control Center, but it was where I was to meet people, particularly an Iraqi man who would change the course of my life. It was this good man who would teach me to respect Islam, Muslims, and Iraqi culture. He would humanize the Iraqi people in a way that would dash, all of the dehumanization the Army had tried to pound into me during my training.

His name was Ali, a common name for a Shiite Muslim. Twenty people would come forward. Perhaps it is fitting that he would have a common name; for me, he and those of his work crew would come to represent the ordinary people of Iraq. People who I found I had to disagreements with whatsoever. He was short, shorter than my five feet eight inches. He loved Eminem, and all things American. He always wore the same clothing, so you could always pick him out in the crowd. Then again, the workers almost always wore the same clothes, as if it was all they owned. He was despite the lessons he taught me, not a devout Muslim. He wanted to come to the United States very badly, and experience the world. I didn't think he had ever traveled out of Dhi Qar province. He was however a man with kind eyes, and man who you felt you could trust, even though you were not supposed to. There was a simple humanity to his eyes, and that is what I recall the most about him. He was ordinary in every sense of the word, but he held the decency of common humanity in him. There was no hatred or malice in him, he was an open man, ready to accept new ideas and concepts from the outside world. Perhaps it was fitting that before the De-Baathification ordered by our Viceroy L. Paul Bremer, he had been a teacher.

      Now he was a servant of the occupation, not something all of the Iraqis in this crowded area, of foreign words, and smells were happy to be. In the mist of hundreds of them were about twenty Americans, in full gear, looking for their team of workers. To this day I cannot stand crowds, although over the years I have gotten better. I used to panic, I would hate to be next to Muslims in a crowd, and they would terrify me. I remember thinking walking into the Visitor Control Area, when are they going to realize there are hundreds of them and only a few of us. Thankfully that day never came, but the thought bothered me then, as it does now. Why didn't they attack? I had been almost sure they would.

We would gather the workers and badge them. These badges would indicate that the workers had permission to be on the base escorted by a member of the US military. As far as I know, we were the only ones who used Iraqi labor. I do not know that for sure, but I don't recall seeing any of our coalition partners there when we did our morning pickups.

Ali was a local, from Nasiriya 20 kilometers up the main highway from Cob Adder. He always wore the same baseball cap of the Iraqi national football team, and the same grey shirt. He was the only member of the group of workers that spoke English, as he had been a school teacher before the war. When Paul Bremer ordered the de-baathification, under direction from President Bush, he had lost his job as a public-school teacher. He was reduced to performing manual labor for the US military, but he never seemed bitter about it. He hated Saddam very much and told me he remembered the crackdown on Shiite Muslims after the first gulf war, when president Bush 41 had urged the Iraqi people to rise up against Saddam, and then watched the wholesale slaughter of thousands.

Now that his nation had fallen, he seemed determined that he was going to help Iraqi stabilize and become a better place. He longed for America as well and wished nothing more than to be a citizen. He had a love of American culture that can only be expressed by people in the developing world. We take things for granted in the west, Ali did not. He loved Eminem, all Hip Hop, in fact, and would always ask questions about the United States. He was trying to get someone to sponsor him to come to the united states as a refugee, perhaps because he could tell what was coming. We left him there at the end of our tour. I never found out what happened to him. I often wonder if he has been swept up in the fight against ISIS, which has pitted local militias and the Iraqi Army against the Islamic State and its tribal allies in Al-Anbar. I wonder if he was beheaded or, tortured for being a collaborator when we pulled out in 2011. COB Adder was the last base we occupied in Iraq before the 2011 end of the war, Ali would have been working there until the very end if he had lived that long. Working for the Americans was not always the most popular thing for an Iraqi to do after all.

  The team of workers we had were good men and boys. At first, I did not trust them at all. I assumed that all Iraqis we terrorists and that we had to be on guard. There was a list of things that the

Iraqis could not bring on base for that very reason. The military did not want the workers conducting espionage for the insurgency. I eventually found them to be poor people merely trying to support their families, but I wondered sometimes if they were working for the other side. I still do. One thing I know for sure is that I wish I had taken more pictures. I have no pictures of Ali and me, but he is the Iraqi I remember most. He is a person I remember most fondly, who changed my opinion of the middle east and Islam. As our tour went on, we would speak a great deal, and he would teach me Arabic, and I would improve his English, which was much better than my Arabic. Ali was not particularly religious, but we discussed religion as well. He seemed to have a very multicultural view of the world, not worrying too much about the convention, or what was expected of him.

The worker's job was to build up addition to our ASP, or ammunition supply point. On the days we would pick them up, they would have an old man with a blue "bongo truck" come on base, carrying tools and equipment, his name was Dachil, and his *misbaḥah* hangs above my desk as I write this accounting. He was a man who spoke little English, but always had a kind and happy disposition. He was kind and honest, one could see it without even looking that hard at him. He was also a man who had lived through Saddam's regime and the sanctions that had come later. He had been a MIG fighter pilot in Saddam's Air Force and flew out of the base on which he now did manual labor for the Americans. When we would drive by the air strip, he would look longingly at it, point and say, "I Fly, now I am Driver." He had retired from Saddam's government, for his service, but had lost it when the government in Baghdad had fallen. As a result, he had been forced by necessity to working for the Americans.

Despite Dachil having every good reason to be angry or resentful of Americans in general, and our military especially, I learned a valuable lesson from my interactions with him. If a person does not act superior and treats everyone with respect, only the most hateful person and return your kindness with scorn. Dachil was always kind to me, bringing me Samoon, or Iraqi flatbread every day I saw him, along with a carbonated orange soda with the pulp still in it. He knew I was just a kid, far away from home, and he knew I was lonely. He would drive behind our 5-ton truck every day, and follow us to the ammunition supply point (ASP). After going through the main facility, past the gate guards at our ASP, we would pull off into the empty desert, between the ASP and the security fence; this is what they would transform from a desolate wasteland of sand, into storage for weapons of war.

  The Iraqis worked very hard every day. The projects they worked on were valued at $250,000 US Dollars. What they were paid to an exact number, I am unsure, but you can bet it was not comparable. Exploitation takes many forms, and the poor and desperate span the globe. The only thing that changes in that equation is the level of exploitation. Being paid very little by an occupying force, to build up their capacity to occupy your country is sure to be humiliating. But they gave me a fucking medal for it. No shit, it was mentioned in my citation write up for the army commendation medal. Poor and working-class people in one country are sent to exploit poor and working people in another country. That does not sit well with me. If it sits well with you, then I feel sorry for you.

These things cannot sit well with me because I worked with these people. I sat among them while they ate, and they laughed like people I knew at home. They would share their food with me, something that I treasured, more than gold. Through them, I came to understand Islam and Arabic culture and found it to have some of the same values, and the culture I grew up in. Our similarities can unite us. They must unless we want, or can accept perpetual war.

I often wonder about my personal responsibility for deaths caused during my time in Iraq. A VA therapist once told me that I cannot hold myself reasonable for the war itself. After all, senior officials and officers have command responsibility. That seems to me to be a truth and a convenient excuse at the same time. I cannot totally absolve myself of all wrongdoing. As I have become a peaceful man since the war, my responsibility is all too clear to me.

We can see from several studies that the people of Iraq are suffering from birth defects, the likes of which the world has not seen since Hiroshima.[iii] The cause of this should be clear to anyone who is paying attention. US weapons are causing birth defects. As a former ammunition specialist, what is my culpability in civilian deaths? Fallujah is just the tip of the iceberg.[iv] We know that depleted uranium is a staple in munitions that has horrible effects and has a half-life of 4.5 billion years.[v] We must examine the policies of our government and military action if we ever want to pass on a stable, viable, livable world to future generations.

I often wonder how it must have felt for them to be working for an occupying army that had taken their country by force, and I don't believe myself unpatriotic for wondering such things. If, for example, the Chinese had taken over my home state of New York, I think the locals would be more than just a little resentful, despite any claims that it was to liberate us.[vi] Some of the workers were much more resentful than others. Some openly gave us dirty looks, and institutional racism was present on our side, although, in my unit, we had a majority of good honorable and tolerant people.

The questions I ask and the problems I raise with the occupation have nothing to do with the actions of my unit in particular. The 962ndnd Ordnance Company and the 77th Sustainment Brigade were decent and honorable soldiers, who did their duty without so much as a violation of the Iraqi people's human dignity, the policies of our national government, however, cannot be so easily and truthfully defended. One cannot excuse the occupation of Iraq. Some say was a war of aggression, fought without United Nations sanction. That cannot be swept under the rug, nor can the deaths of 4,400 US troops, or the wide-ranging estimates of Iraqi civilians who were killed, nor can the two million displaced people simply be ignored either.[vii] That is the dilemma I think that anyone who thinks deeply about such issues must come to. Can this war be justified? Should we kill for our governments? Some contemplate this question and say yes, wholeheartedly. I say no with a conviction you could not shake with the greatest of thrashing. War, to me, is a great evil that we must wipe from this earth. It cannot be considered a way of settling disputes with other people. We must evolve past our need for violence, and our tendency towards division if we ever wish to build a better world for future generations.

For my work as a solider, my commander wrote me a memorandum of reference in which he said in part, "Specialist Soel served as an assigned soldier on the Visitor Control Operations Section (VCC), on multiple occasions for over nine months. His duties were to provide force protection for fellow soldiers at the Supply point and to advise and assist local Iraqi government contractor's daily operations at the supply point. Spc. Soel's team oversaw the successful completion of multiple government contracting projects totaling more than $250,000 in the operations area."

There were workers at the airbase from all over the world, and it made the place a small city in the empty desert. Workers from Bangladesh worked in the DFAC and did laundry for the troops. Some locals could have small shops near the PX or Post exchange where they would sell smokes, bootlegged DVDs, and Iraqi style clothing. There was even a gold store on base. An Irishman ran a shop where you could buy cars. With the massive amounts of money that the soldiers brought in, with almost nowhere to spend it I saved a lot. I avoided most of them because I felt that I should save my money. Saving money did nothing for me when I returned, I was burned out, and while it was great to have thirty-five grand. It means nothing when you are mentally unstable; I spent it in a good year and a half. I spent money on booze like it was going out of style.

Off time on at COB Adder was spent in a myriad of activities when it came. The advantage of being on a large airbase was that we, unlike any troops, had access to a surprising number of amenities. We have many of the comforts of home. Of course, they had the Iraqi shops, selling everything from jewelry bootleg DVDs, some of which I still have. We had life pretty good, despite being in the desert. Being away from home was sometimes the hardest part. A soldier's life can be filled with loneliness. At least that is how I remember it. The Army had set up a trailer with payphones in it, where you could use international calling cards to call home. I called my dad a lot. I told him I was scared sometimes, and we talked about life back in town most of all. He is a veteran of the Vietnam War, reassured me I would be alright. Technology somehow took away from the truthfulness of the experience for me. I have always sought genuine experience and shunned the false. But we had it right, complaining about that would just be ungrateful. I think Tallil/COB Adder was viewed by many in the Army as an "easy tour," because of all the amenities. We even had a hookah bar that was nearly hit in a mortar attack. Thank God they didn't take out Green Bean Coffee.

Writings from Etemenniguru

Chapter Five

I did some writing while I was in Iraq as well. Most of them were poems, and they passed the time when I could not sleep or had a long guard at the gate, and times were slow.

Insomnia My Reenlistment Bonus

I have not been sleeping well. I last posted about my first month in Iraq. But sleep will not come. The sirens are going off, something about a test. Now I'm rolling on the floor and look like a fool, but sometimes I do it out of habit.

Attention Cob Adder

This is a test of the giant voice alert system

This is only a test

The uniform alert level is alert level 3

All non-essential personnel are to remain indoors

That is all

Air raid siren continues blaring

I wonder what it feels like to be blown up. Being shredded to nothing but a mist by mortar would be no way to go out.

So, I lay awake, and I wonder. About the men in civilian clothes who come to my work site as "State department" Kind of funny because their shirt says Triple Canopy. Private contractors, who until recently were not bound by the Uniform Code of Military Justice. I give them ammo. All kinds and types of munitions pass through that gate. They need it to defend themselves. Sickness, to think of the child run over and my friend who I have worried about last week coming back inside the Wire. Dreams, like a fog, daydreams of the road. I flinch on base, sleep, and awake at the wheel, going from briefing to guard to check my screen. Hoping to hear from home. To hear from home is to always know that somewhere in this twisted place, sanity can exist.

Their eyes still haunt me. That is the problem. Not tears but just a look. A that could look not belonging to a three-year-old child. A small boy. No older than my cousin's children, perhaps your children. He runs to me covered in filth, begging for whatever I have. I take out a pill, my prescription to take it, anxiety attack. No time for it now. Must stop it. Must drive on. We have a mission. He begs, his eyes desperate. He speaks not. His hands are as small as can be. Just barely walking. I hand him a pop tart. Which he drops, then eats it covered in mud from the fresh rain. He is shoeless, hungry, not at daycare, not getting ready for kindergarten, but here begging for food. His mother hides behind a wall. She is scared of us I think. She keeps peeking out, and I know she is scared. Why? What have I done but feed her kids? It's probably the 50. Cal gun on our Humvee The gunner laughs. "Hey Soel "that's fucked up, you're not going to eat that pop-tart in front of that kids are you."

"No!" I say, trying to regain my bearings. As a girl of about 8 Again, filthy runs up to me to show me her goat. Small dirty animal. I can feel the pity in my soul writhing out in broken Arabic. Her sister is also there. Her image is also haunting. She points at me and says "Mister, look."

As I do so, I see half of her finger gone. She is asking for a band-aid. I almost puke. Regain my composure and tell her its healed. She just needs to keep it clean.

We mount up.

I feel like I have betrayed my own humanity. What the hell am I doing here?

Not sure of what I should have done, but I only know what I did was not enough.

And so, they will remain in my memory. I wonder how they are doing. If the militias got them. If the small boy I met was the one, a convoy ran over I had heard about. Oh, that wasn't in the news? Of course not, we need to show the good stories

Win the hearts and minds

If we kill them, all they won't have hearts and minds to win.

I tell my doctor, he gives me more pills. He says, "You don't worry; this guilt you feel is a symptom of depression. You're not a murderer. You were doing your duty. Troops need ammo. These people choose to live this way. We are doing them a favor. You'll be fine, take your meds. And don't worry, you can still re-enlist."

So, insomnia is a reenlistment bonus. This what I draw from my conversation with the good doc. But I most likely will God knows I have a few other options. I mean, these just no work out there. That's what the briefings say. Guess it's a lie.

"Once the nightmares come, they'll throw you away."

More like, once the bad dreams come, they'll toss you some pills.

This is the only movie I know where the zombies have guns.

I even managed to get a bit political, writing to the Stars and Stripes

'Don't ask' a slap to patriots

I praise Stars and Stripes for its article on the "don't ask don't tell" policy hearings ("Households 'don't ask' hearing, first since '93," July 25).

In my view, this policy has hurt our military readiness, hurt the morale of the estimated 65,000 lesbian/gay/bisexual/transgender troops serving around the world, including in the Iraq and Afghanistan theaters of war. It does a disservice to them, as it says to them you can join, you can risk your life, and you can die, and many have, I'm sure, but you cannot: 1. Do it as yourself, and 2. Have the same protection under the law when you get home.

It also shuns the children and same-sex partners of these beautiful people, for they cannot receive the flag as a funeral honor as it is bestowed upon "traditional" families as "thanks from a grateful nation," since the warrior's relationship to them cannot be known.

I feel in long-overdue time, these people will have their justice. The military will have a black mark the likes of which it may take 60 years to recover from, as the recent anniversary of desegregation in the ranks shows. These gay and lesbian heroes serve a nation that gives them neither the comfort of freedom, nor the time of day, and I, for one, thank them for their service in defense of the freedom of others that they cannot enjoy themselves. And they do so in total silence.

Specialist Joseph Soel
Camp Adder, Iraq

This particular opinion piece generated a lot of praise from guys in my unit, but a massive backlash from the Stars and Stripes reading community. I had responses from all over theater by next edition, telling me how wrong I was about the "Don't ask Don't Tell policy". I had to be careful writing it, as I could have been drummed out of the service for being Bisexual, but I'm pretty sure that everyone in the unit knew anyhow. Still, the Army's culture was in flux, and one never knew if you were saying the wrong thing. You had to be careful at the time. Thankfully, with President Obama's repeal of the policy, I was proven correct. At the time, however, the repeal of the policy was no sure thing.

I had brought a small library with me when I went to Iraq. Books have always held exceptional value to me, and I think that life is incomplete without them. I had brought with me "Walden" by

Henry David Thoreau, "A People's History of The United States," by Howard Zinn, and of course my Holman "Soldier's Bible". I still own these books, as they hold the power of the place for me now. Books can do that, books can remind us, and connect us back to our humanity when we feel completely cut off from everything that has been with us in the past. They can be an anchor in the storm, as you roll on waves, from one new place to another, tossed by the will of the sea. Sometimes you felt lost. Sometimes even when people who had become your friends are with you, you felt alone. Books helped with that. They were an escape.

Red River Forty Four: The Day the Sky Fell

Chapter Six

The day Red River 44 went down; I was unaware of its fall. As an ammunition specialist on COB Adder, we were most likely off duty and sleeping. Seven men were inside the CH-47. God rest their souls, and God comfort their families. They were never to reach Balad airbase. To this day, CH-47'S fill me with sadness. They were the only casualties of the Iraq war that I had any direct experience with, and as such, I will never forget their names, which I learned later on.

RIP Red River 44

CPT Robert Vallejo

CWO Brady J. Rudolf

CWO 2 Corry Edwards

Sgt Major Julio Ordonez

Staff Sgt Luke Mason

SGT Daniel Eshbaugh

CPL Michael E. Thompson

      It all hit a bit close to home for me. Our unit went to their dignified transfer ceremony and watched them go by holding a solemn salute. God forgive me I had survived so far. I felt like a coward for having been assigned to the base, while they were out on transit from Kuwait. I would think so again so many times over the preceding years. God forgive me for how can I go on living when so many died. How can I live for 4,448 men and women? God forgive me I will age, time will pass me by, and I hope I will die an old man, and prayerfully peaceably. They will remain young forever, frozen by their right honorable offer laid upon the altar of freedom, and for the love of their friends.

      The official army report cites mechanical failure, no enemy action reported. They were buried together in a veteran's cemetery in Texas. I often think of making my own pilgrimage there. I feel I owe the trip to them. I spent many years guilty that they had died, and I had not. I drank a lot. I did a lot of drugs. I tried to numb myself, as I was more sensitive than most folks. I can take no shame in that as it only a fact of my condition. That guilt may seem illogical to some. But I consider the brotherhood of soldiers as a serious matter, and to me, the only way to take it seriously is to mourn the loss of family. I always do a shot for the fallen on Memorial Day, and still, have a drink for every member of the Red River 44 crew on September 17th. That is my truth, and I suppose it can be no one else's.

  Red River 44 would stay in my mind for years to come, and she still does. I live very near to Fort Lewis Washington now, and every time I hear a CH-47 go overhead, as they often do, I run out to my porch to look at them. It is a reaction I cannot totally explain, but it happens every time nonetheless. CH-47s fill me with a sense of deep sadness, and they never fail to take me back to the experience of Iraq, and the memory of those lost. Those poor guys, those poor fucking guys. I cry for them, even now, and I have no shame in admitting it. The fact that I lived, and they did not, is the thing that drives me to try to achieve as much as I can, they call to me from beyond, reminding me to find the joy, reach higher, love better, and to be a better friend. That is all I can do for them, and it took me a long time to realize that I must do the best I can. Wallowing does no good. Drinking does not help, and the guilt never really goes away.

I was at their "ramp ceremony," also called a "dignified transfer" a military tradition taking the bodies of the fallen home, as we watched their caskets go by, I died a bit inside myself. I felt guilty that my plane would leave from the same airport in a week to go on my leave. I felt a pang of guilt when I flew home for the last time. A part of me died with them. They are who I remember on Memorial Day, they are who I try to honor in my everyday life. I drank a lot to forget those days, and the shame of coming back alive when so many had perished, dying terrible deaths, and for what? I cannot say. I try to believe that everyone who was killed in Iraq died for freedom. That is where my religious ideas about the war and my identity as a soldier an identity is impossible to wash off come into deep conflict. What I can say for sure, is that those lost died for their friends. I can think of hardly a more noble thing than that. They went answered the call of our nation and believed wholeheartedly in their mission. One thing people don't realize is that the military is full of idealists. People who would give up everything to make a positive difference in the world. Often times, our political leaders choose a different course, and war often demands at times that we do bad things or things that are against our better judgment.

So what shall I do now that I have survived? It took me a long time, but I decided to live. I decided to go one and make the world a better place. If not for any other reason than to honor the dead. We veterans, I think, if I may be so presumptuous as to speak for every veteran, must live to those who did not come home. We can see the epidemic of veteran homelessness, a problem which many a government agency is apt to do lip service to ending. Most of this, I think, at least in combat veterans have to do with PTSD and survivor's guilt. I have tried to go on by going to college, falling in love, and writing this book, which I hope will remove the pain from my body. The dead deserve to be remembered. Official ceremonies hold no value for most ordinary people I have known. What they want is to be honored by the long, happy life of those who loved them. I cannot ease the grief of the families of the fallen, but I can tend to my own. Every time I meet a gold star family, I tell them how sorry I am. I beg them to forgive me for being alive. I cannot be ashamed of being real, because in truth I am ashamed of being alive.

What can we say, for those who have lost everything dear to them in war? That is a question that is often overlooked or is provided lip service by government officals every Memorial Day. We cannot ever hope to understand the loss of a gold star family As I sit here on this Memorial Day weekend, I think of all the Barbeques and celebrations that will be taking place. I want to participate, and I often do, but sometimes it feels hollow to me. I want to be a full participant in these celebrations, and in the world at large, but I feel cut off. I am lost in the mirage. Lost to the past sometimes. I remember those mothers who lost sons, while I am safe and sound, and it pains me. The guilt I feel is sometimes too much to deal with. Memorial Day since Iraq, has had a very bittersweet test to me, and that is something I have yet to shake off.

Getting on the Freedom Bird

Chapter Seven

We walked on the tarmac, loaded under what seemed like hundreds of pounds of gear. We were tired and happy at the same time. It had been a lot of hard monotonous labor to get to this point. There had been heartache, loneliness, friendship, and loss. We were finally going home, the "freedom bird" loomed before us. As we walked out of the "Terminal", nothing like an airport terminal you would see in the United States, we passed two Iraqi men, filling sandbags. "As-salāmu alaykum" I had said to them, may God's peace be upon you, and they smiled. I was saying goodbye to the people of Iraq. My last words in Iraq were to wish some Iraqi men peace. Did I even have the right?

We had been awarded our medals the previous day, Army Commendation or Achievement Medals by the Battalion Commander, and our Iraq Campaign Medals by our company commander. I had finally earned something that I had longed to, a campaign medal. I would do my dad proud, but was I proud? I felt proud, but something wasn't quite right. He had earned the Vietnam Campaign Medal, and I had seen it, stashed in his toolbox, when I was a kid. He kept them in the shed, away from anyone's view, including himself. I to would put my war in a box, for a long time, I would neither speak of it, nor glory in it. But there was a sadness building in me, it was something I could not control. I felt lost. I didn't know what to do, and It has taken a long time for me to feel a shred of balance, as I do now. For a long time, I would drink, and very heavily so, to try to numb the sadness I had brought back with me. I still don't feel that I have fully integrated back to regular society.

We flew from Iraq to Ali Salem Air Base in Kuwait, and the waiting began for a flight to get home. I wasn't sure I was ready, but it was coming. I was excited, and scared, and happy, and sad, everything felt like a whirlwind. We spent a lot of time wandering around the holding area, smoking. They had established it as a no salute zone, which I think served everyone just fine. We were all tired, officers, and enlisted both. We of course, being citizen soldiers, ready to take off the uniform and shed some of the restrictions of Army life. It had been a year without beer for us, and we wanted that drink badly.

After coming home, I fell headfirst into addiction. The drinking would begin as soon as I got back. I was finally old enough to go to bars, and that would be my downfall. I would spend one hundred dollars a night easily on booze. Drinking four to five long islands at a time. Depression had gotten ahold of me, and I felt lost, totally, and completely lost. Binge drinking became a comfort and a curse for me, and the booze barley helped to numb the pain of what I felt I had participated in. People like to view things in black and white, but some know there is a lot of grey in the world. My self-esteem, not being so high before the war, had been shattered. I had no idea what I was supposed to do with my life or where I was supposed to go. So, I migrated from barstool to barstool. Back-alley, to back-alley smoking weed. Always trying to stay high, chasing the next buzz. Beer cans littered the floor of a small one-bedroom I had rented on the east side of town. My life was a disintegrating mess for those first few years, the addiction, and the abuse of alcohol and drugs lasted for ten years.

    I can feel the urge now, as I contemplate the depths of my addiction. I have cut back and avoided rehab, but at the time of rock bottom, inpatient treatment seemed the only thing that I could consider dealing with my issues. Time has numbed the pain, like scar tissue over an old wound, but it still stings deep within. The desert gets into your soul, and war can affect people in different ways. After the war I no longer believed in God and viewed the world through dark glasses. I would sit on unemployment and wait for the bar to open. I had degenerated into a drunk and felt the pain of failure daily. Sometimes I still feel it in the wee hours of the morning when I wake up from a bad dream. It took me almost a decade to feel a sense of normality, and even now, real progress alludes me. I feel as though I have been left behind sometimes. Left out of the game if you like. I'm glad God believed in me because he lifted me out of my circumstances.

I went to a few VA therapists when I got home, and some even seemed to give a shit, the VA was a mess then, still in a pre-war footing, so to speak. It's like they had not anticipated, bitter former soldiers coming in on mass for help. Pills were the answer then and still are today. I take five of them. One for sleep and one for nightmares. One for depression and two for anxiety. My VA rating is at eighty percent, which affords me a decent amount to live on at least, but even with a disability, I feel worthless a lot of the time. I fear getting to forty and realizing I have accomplished nothing. That, I think, is why some veterans hold on to their war, even when it causes them extreme pain. If the war is all you have to be proud of, you hug it like an old friend and wear it on your sleeve. The VA also gave me pain pills and muscle relaxers, they are for fibromyalgia and chronic pain. My medical marijuana card helps, as well. I hear stories of other Iraq veterans, who have similar problems coming down with cancer. This scares me.

I seek solace in religion but can find none. The only relief I see comes from a bottle. I try Alcoholics anonymous, I quit. I had a 24 hours serious coin, I keep it, but you cannot buy booze with it. Addiction is a cycle and one that I have not yet escaped. I started smoking cigarettes in Iraq and am now hopelessly addicted, and cannot stop, even when I will myself too. My will has been defeated. Getting sober will be a challenge for me even now, so far removed from the desert. God forgive me, but self-loathing plays a part. Hatred of the self can be the most destructive force in our lives, I can serve as proof of that. I turn to poetry to get the pain out of me; it might work better than booze and nicotine. You go from sober to drunk and back again.

Payment

America send me your children.

The sand will swallow them.

Saddam promised, "Iraq will be your graveyard."

Do you hear the desert calling?

"Why do you hesitate, send your children to me."

"I have swallowed the armies of a great many empires."

You come seeking liberation.

But the desert offers no such thing.

It goes on beyond any horizon.

Your children will be lost here.

Their Ghosts are calling out to go home.

Their bodies will return, the spirit shall remain.

The desert claims payment from all who venture here.

Send your children America, send them unto me.

Forgiveness

You seek solace in a bottle.

Find yourself in the bubbles if you can.

Forgive yourself, with a shot of crown.

Jack is not listening.

The captain is calling.

Your old self is loathing you.

Can you drown him in cheap beer?

Light up a smoke to shield you from yourself.

Hide in the chemicals, and shove it down another level.

Check yourself before you wreck yourself, and pay your tab

We all have to pay our tab

The bar always closes, and loneliness returns.

Drinking buddies never care; are they your friends?

Last call buddy, you can't stay here.

Give me another beer.

Last call loser, get out

I used to be someone

I used to walk tall and proud

They applauded me in airports, now they scoff at me in gutters

God, forgive me?

Can you forgive yourself? Could you do more?

*Can we forgive ourselves for our perceived failures? Can we forgive ourselves for surviving? In my case, anyway, I have always felt that my pathetic life could never live up to the experiences that might have been lived by those we lost. The question of why did I come home often comes to mind, and morphs into, why did I deserve to go back, when so many others, probably worthier did not. It all seems too random to chalk it up to anything but dumb luck.

Seven Shots

Seven shots, lined up in formation

crush my pain with cheap libations

Give me captain to remember the captain.

Merry men are we!

Seven men who went down

Live for them.

When living gets to hard drink for them.

Merry men are we!

So line 'em up and drink em down

For men who never made it home

Cause life's not fair

You can't let them go

You can't move on

*Every year on Memorial Day I have seven shots, which makes for a terrible hangover. So I had to change it to seven drinks of various kinds, mostly beer. I do it to memorialize the soldiers killed in a helicopter crash in Iraq on September 18th, 2008.

Inner Peace with PBR

Jukebox music lulls you away

PBR cold metallic taste

Cigarette smoke fills your lungs

and life spills out of you onto the page

You traveled far from your home

A roamer and a rambler

Dive bar dreams and a life of regret

So much to do, but a game of pool sounds good

I will not get drunk today

I WILL NOT GET DRUNK TODAY

Considering life goes better with beer

If I get this poison out of me, I'll be better off.

St. Frankie's Bar and Grill

The past 10 years have been full of pain

Combat boots on the pavement.

We were worshiped as heroes, remember?

Gods among men, if you believe the propaganda

We were hailed in the congress

"God bless our troops."

We were abandoned on our own streets

"Hey, buddy, spare a dollar?"

Reality TV moved on without us

We could not forgive ourselves

We got lost in the maze of our great cities

So, we found directions in a bottle

Forgiveness in a toke

The beer goes down easy

Life stays hard

but A.A was not for us.

So we go to Saint Frankie's

for a drink and confessional

We were once heroes to be praised

When you trade-in your cammies for a veteran hat

They throw you away.

They say "Thank you for your service" on Veterans Day

And we go forward into the world, only to fight the VA.

Veterans Affairs, please hold.

Thank you for calling the Department of Veterans Affairs

If you are having a physical or mental health emergency

Please hang up and dial 911

If you are having thoughts of hurting yourself

Please call the veteran's crisis line at 1-800-442-8255.

Sorry, all representatives are currently assisting other veterans,

Please remain on the line, and your call will be answered in the order

it was received.

My Veteran Experience

Chapter Eight

Looking back and remembering is a funny thing.

Sometimes when one beer isn't enough, so you reach for one more.

Looking back on beer downed, and Soldiers who can't order one anymore.

Not drinking seems like a slight against those men.

In the desert, I turned twenty-one. I better make up for that lost year.

What am I doing here; I guess it wasn't my time yet.

Why can't I put this bottle down then?

I'm sorry I survived, and I'm so sorry your sons had to die.

My experience as a veteran has mixed, and while some in older generations of veterans may say, "You have to pick yourself up by your bootstraps and drive on" that is not so easy to do in real life sometimes. There is a vast grey area to experience that we forget about when idealizing the reactions, we think we are supposed to have, to a given set of circumstances.

I came home in January 2008, and was quite the mess, to be perfectly honest. Depression had dogged me since my time overseas, just because of the sheer loneliness of the experience, that readjusting was very hard. I felt alone in a crowded room, very out of place. I remember at a house party in Rochester, New York, I stood with a friend of mine who had also deployed. We looked at each other awkwardly, as what I can only describe as hipsters danced around me. I longed to belong to the carefree world again, but that was proving very difficult for me. And the drinking got worse over time.

With thirty-five thousand dollars in the bank from my deployment, the money went easy, just like a Staff Sergeant had told me it would, for a little while he had said. I had lost my faith in God, which was so central to my life as a child, and a young adult. I had lost many of a misconception, being formerly a republican, and believing wholeheartedly in the war I had volunteered for, I had become adrift in a sea of personal confusion. I had no rudder to guide me, and that was perhaps the most disorienting thing of all. I went to all the veteran's centers to get registered and went through the motions of intake appointments. The VA prescribed me Zoloft than, Prozac, and Wellbutrin. Trazodone for sleep, and Prazosin for the nightmares. 600-milligram Ibuprofen for the pain in my knees. As a young man, I was unprepared to deal with the Labyrinthian system that the VA really was.

I spent a lot of time at bars and had been very fond of Nightclubs in Rochester before I deployed, but I found that the crowd scared me when I tried to go back. I tried not to feel bitter, but I felt bitter quite a bit. I still feel angry now, even 8 years removed from the experience. I wonder how the villagers are doing. I wonder how many have been killed.

    The military experience, and especially the war experience, can make people distant from their respective societies. I knew what home was, and I could not accept it, which made me very angry. I went on a binge of drugs and alcohol, meanwhile still showing up for battle assembly, hoping not to be pulled for a random drug test. I somehow missed them. Even being in the army, made my transition to a peace activist very confusing. It made my time in the military very disheartening. While before I had wanted a military career, now I tried to escape as soon as possible. The prospect of being deployed again was always there as well. What scared me the most that I would be sent off to Afghanistan, or Iraq, to wade through the same shit that I had just crawled out of. I started smoking Spice, a conventional drug in the mid-2000s, to replace the marijuana that would have inevitably popped me hot in a drug test. I still wonder what the long-term effects of it will be, but I was a paranoid, strung out the mess, and I had to stop myself from smoking it. It was a very dark time, and how can I convey the time that passed during these events? It was five years, at least. Not a very happy five years, but one that formational for me. Some of the drug experiences I had were quite good.

  I longed for inner peace, and I am still looking for it, I thought of the hippies and thought that is how I really wanted to live my life happy and free, but mental health issues continued to beguile me. I wanted to be positive and free, a free spirit. I wanted to go west. However, I was held on the east coast, by my military assignment, and fear as well. I would have to wait and bide my time. When I look back on it now, it all seems very surreal. It is hard to believe that my life's course evolved like it did.

Because I was in the reserves, I had to work a regular job and live in the local community, which was a real blessing for me actually. I could not have borne being under the army's control all the time. My truest transformation had begun. From soldier to hippie, and an anti-war activist was born as well. I was going to transform myself, the purest expression of which was moving west. Which it would turn out, was the best decision I ever made. I needed to be away from home. I needed to go to the Pacific Ocean.

Lessons Learned

I learned in Iraq, a great many things that perhaps some others didn't. Life is malleable to allow each of us to take different lessons from the same experience. I really like that about life, maybe you do to?

Muslims are not monsters or terrorists. The number of terrorists is minimal, considering the world's one billion Muslims.

Some of the younger Iraqis we worked with were very secular. Like one who took vacations to Jordan, Or Lebanon, I forget which one. In our current climate, with a candidate calling for a total ban on Muslims, we should be cautious. We should screen folks obviously, from everywhere, but to ban an entire religion is anti-American, as well as very cruel. To deny refugee status is to doom a person to roam, it is a sentence to poverty, and to be forever a stranger in a strange land. Chased from one place or another. If another state ran into a natural disaster or an attack, people would say, "of course we will help them, they are Americans" But are we not all human beings, all family? If we cannot love members of our own family, who can we love? The workers that I got to know in Iraq were beautiful people, some of the finest I have ever met in fact. They welcomed me to eat with them and shared their food happily. I asked questions and learned about their culture, their religion, and them as people.

    They accepted their situation with grace and humility, and with joy in so many cases. There are, in fact, Iraqi refugees who would be welcome in my home. That does not mean we can sacrifice security entirely, and just let in waves of them. We should be welcoming, but cautious, because they are some bad folks as well, which the Iraqis and Syrians do not want in their country. The terrorists, whose perversion of Islam shames them, have killed more Muslims than non-Muslims. They are a death cult, and no decent person wants a death cult to cut down their family, or anyone else's. We need to stop the hype and stop the hate.

      The dehumanization of the enemy in the army was ever prevalent. I'm sure that the Department of the Army will deny it, as well as those still stuck in the military mentality, but hatred exists. Hatred of outsiders and those of the Islamic faith does exist. Crusader imagery is present and used by those in the military of a Born Again Christian persuasion to frame the war on terror as a holy war. Even those staunch defenders of the faith mean well, some more anti-war folks may be shocked to hear me say. But they genuinely believe that there is a clash of civilizations going on and that they are defending us from grave danger. In a way we are. I have no doubt that terrorism is a thing to be guarded against, but I question the extent and our reaction. I question our role in creating terrorists as well. The war has not been a good thing. Revenge breeds revenge, hatred brings more hatred. Why we have not learned this as a species yet, I do not understand.

So, do I have peace? Did I find it? I honestly don't know. We don't see the peace I think, it is a journey, not a destination that we reach. We find little happiness every now and again, a little comfort. Mostly I think we just struggle day by day. What am I to do with that? What will you? Perhaps you find it dissatisfying, well welcome to my world. Or rather welcome to the world. Because this book took so long for me to finish, I think I have evolved while writing it. That is true of any book but especially in my case, of this one.

I have found sobriety, I can tell you that, but the raw pain that I started this book with has somewhat subsided over the years. It only really comes up when something triggers it, like a smell, sound, or a memory. It used to sting, and now it is just a dull pain in my soul, but I must go on despite it. I am still anti-war, but not because I am a communist, or a socialist, or a democrat. I have become more libertarian in my old age, not that you care what party box I check on election day, but because it is in line with my principles, and if you have read this far, and traveled this road with me then perhaps you care somewhat for what my principals are. We shall continue to be at war in the middle east I am afraid. We cannot seem to get out of our military adventures as a country. No matter what party we elect we find that out sons and daughters are dying in wars overseas. Seventeen years after the 9/11 attacks we are still at war. We have begun to ignore it as a country. We have become numb to it, and it has ceased to affect us unless we know someone who is there. Most damning we have become accustomed to it. The casualties have gone down because our "allies," some would say puppets are doing the dying for us. What can be done about this? We cannot seem to vote our way out of the issue.

    I fear we may have to go broke as a country before the war ends, and the troops come home. To be quite honest, I was afraid to even try to publish this, in part because of fears of rejection, and in fear of being a traitor by the nationalist elements who have taken power in recent years. After all, this work began when George W. Bush was president. In short, what I have discovered is that nationalist fervor is not the way, and neither is militant opposition to all national unity. The radical middle is where I must stand because I can find no other morally justifiable ground upon which to stake my claim. I love America so much I am still willing to die for the nation if the need arises, but I will not be a man-made tool for the purposes of ambitious or immoral men. I don't really want to fight anymore, but I believe in America. I believe in our institutions and I believe in freedom, love, and peace. I'm more of a Gary Johnson Libertarian.

Memorial Day

I remember those men who did not make it back.

They are with me always, always right at my back.

They whisper to me to not forget them

"You have to live every day as if it were my last"

I feel the pain of their loss, and I know I have to go on

There is nothing I can do about them being gone

I lived, and they died, what can I do?

So I stand at attention to offer a salute

Don't wish me a happy Memorial Day!

It's a day of reflection for me

In your life, stop and remember them

Because I can't forget them

Stuck in these boots

I can't just put those men away in those boxes

Sand whips by us, and it feels like a cold night

It must be 65 degrees

We stand erect, at perfect attention

Our shadows are carried by in boxes

They are men who we might not have liked in life

We don't even know their names at present

But there we stand, our bodies aching from holding that same hand salute

The flag-draped coffins, red white, and blue

The Chaplin offers a prayer

How in the Fuck did we get here?

I feel stuck in my boots, and I WANT OUT!!!

That should be me in that box, I fucking know it

I can never live it down, I can't move

So I'll just stand here, saluting, on this tarmac in the middle of the

night

For the rest of my life

Playing Soldier

You got to play soldier for real kid

That's how it feels, that one time you escaped the FOB

I didn't have to go, so that's got to count for something

One guy watched outside of his "store" more of a shack, really

His eyes squint in the sun. But there is hate in them

He looks right at me. Menacingly

My finger moves and a flash

He's frozen in time now, glaring at me

His grey shirt is wind-whipped

He looks tired and determined

Years later, I look at the picture

Four more men lurked in the darkness, all staring us down

I wonder if they were planning an attack or just watching.

Part of me wishes they had so I could have proven myself

But we drove on by. No one died that day

Tea with Wadood

The fire is made from pieces of pallets.

They burn hot, even with the sun beating us down.

Iraqi Tea, at least as I experienced it and came to know it

It was a precious thing. Chai, they called it.

I sought it out and would drink Tea with the Iraqis at every opportunity

Wadood would make the fire with care, Boil the water, and leaves.

As far as I was concerned, being offered tea was a very high honor.

Long Distance with a Gold Star Father

Corporal Thompson's father called me on my back balcony.

It was early autumn, and the leaves were just beginning to fall.

I told him how sorry I was that his son had died and I had survived

I told him I had been carrying this weight around with me for 10 years.

I begged him to forgive me for surviving. I was asking his permission to be alive

He took everything I said in stride. He was a veteran himself.

He relieved me of the weight he said his son would not have wanted me to carry.

He told me that I could put it down. I was finally free.

Put down that weight, but I left it in the corner of my office.

I keep his son, and all the fallen in the forefront of my mind.

As I work for veterans causes, I do so for them.

I offer my life as a living monument to their loss.

Before we hung up, he thanked me for helping to bring his son home.

All I had done was stand and salute.

I assured him that Mikey had been escorted and honored by his brothers and sisters.

As holy as the flag or the cross, the war dead shall be borne up

Held up on high for all to see their glory.

That we might not enter a war too earnestly. But hold peace dearly in our hearts.

He told me his son had died for his friends.

I know that he died for me.

It could have been me just as quickly.

For a long time, I felt it should have been me.

Now that I have permission to continue mission from

A man whose sandals I am not worthy to untie

I will work to honor his family's sacrifice.

Here's to the boys we lost in that Desert.

May we never forget them.

Wake up and get moving

Shoot for whatever goal you have

Do it for Mikey

That's what I do

I can't leave him now

I could have if we had just passed each other in an airport.

A stranger

Although he is a stranger, still I will never leave him

I will hold his memory in my mind so that I might ensure

He is never forgotten.

Saint Michael Archangel,

Defend us in battle,

(You'd better have my back)

be our protection against the wickedness and snares of the devil;

May God rebuke him, we humbly pray;

and do thou, O Prince of the heavenly host,

by the power of God, cast into hell

Satan and all the evil spirits.

who prowl through the world seeking the ruin of souls.

Amen

(Don't fucking let me die.)

Shadow Mirror

You'll wake up and go out to the balcony to have a smoke. The darkness will be a mirror.

All the things you did or failed to do will be at the rage in your mind's eye.

How could you be living inside your mind's eye? This dream needs to go away.

Boom! Wake up! Run! Were you even that scared at the time?

"Wheres your body armor soldier"?

"On the Truck Sarnt," you reply.

Better go get it, don't fucking die.

You run again, heart pounding.

Don't fucking die, don't fucking die.

You grab it and throw your Kevlar on your head.

Carrying your 16.4-pound armor. It feels heavier.

Did the sand suddenly get faster? Yeah, this must be quicksand.

You cross the threshold of the bunker, like a guy who just won the Boston marathon.

A few minutes later, the all-clear is sounded.

You will be "smoked" in your full gear, waiting for the next mortar to hit.

At that exact moment, the bunker, your armor, even the wire is meaningless.

You are waiting for your turn. They say you don't hear the one that gets you.

I am Still waiting for it.

"Learn from it and drive the fuck on!"

We suffer together

A Soldier and I run through the sand.

We guard a deserter at Fort Knox. He's pretending to be crazy, we are told.

Am I crazy?

Shoot them if they go past such and such a landmark in the open Desert.

Beat your face until you die!

Hi, I'm Joe, and I'm an alcoholic.

VCC-4915

7601-4753

Would you have the good name here, if you came unarmed?

I look at my Iraq Campaign medal.

When I was young, I saw my dad's Campaign Medal

I wanted to earn one myself

Now I chug my beer and scream silently

I stare at it. I stare at my medal.

WHAT AM I SUPPOSED TO DO WITH TIIS?!?

Oh God, it fucking hurts!

How am I supposed to go on when so many died?

I can't wash this off.

I can't live this down.

I feel useless now that I am not saluting you passing caskets,

I never wear it. It sits in a box

I never wear it, and I cannot take it off.

If I quit drinking how will I feel?

If I stopped drinking how will I cry for them?

I go to the A.A. meeting.

I drink coffee

All I want is a drink

Cold and refreshing

Quitting would be easier

If only coffee could taste like beer.

Odysseus at Etemenniguru

Chapter Nine

Sing to me Libertas, of the city

Destroyed by fire, a nation burned

Choking on phosphorus gas, survivors

Crying bitter tears, Screaming

Into the Arabian night

Tell me of a man

Lost in the sands

Of time

Bound for Ithaca

He was blown off course

By angry Poseidon

Landing in the Levant, his ship smashed he wandered

The wastelands, closer to Ilium than home

Falling to his knees at the

The foot of a great temple he cried

"Whatever gods may rule this cursed place

Deliver me from wind and sand

Save me from this fate

Doomed to die a wretched death

So far from hearth and home."

Shining Nanna

Heard his call and left

Her charges, the Shepherd boys,

Watering their sheep in the

The life-giving Euphrates

Nanna, holy goddess of the moon

Called to him,

"Take Heart weary wayfarer,

Indeed no one has suffered more than you.

I shall host you in my inner sanctum

My waters shall refresh your spirit

My food shall soothe your soul

Come, and rest your bones,

Noble Greek. The journey from here

To your home is far too perilous now

Come rest a while, I will bear you up."

Following the fair goddess

Odysseus climbed the grand steps of

The Ziggurat, Etemenniguru

UR of the Chaldeans, a great city

at his back.

Nanna: Tricking the Trickster

Nanna led Odysseus through her temple,

Mudbrick walls adorned with tiles

Shining in the sun.

"Fair Odysseus," she said,

"A haboob will blow in from the gulf,

I can sense it.

Angry Poseidon seeks your death."

Odysseus replied,

"He may try, oh, holy one

No one is better at not dying than I!"

As Odysseus ate his fill,

One on Nanna's handmaidens brought a bowl

Mixed in it some spiced wine and

With a gentle hand,

caused the old soldier to drink deeply.

Looking to him with pity Nanna said,

"Old Warrior, Hero of Troy,

One more fight you must endure.

A time so far from now requires your attention.

For now, sleep, and I shall guide you through."

His eyes drooping, Odysseus gave way to sleep.

Nanna ordered her servants to place him in room

Blankets, a beautiful couch safe from the storm.

Now, with great power, she sealed the room

Walled off, encased in sand and time

Odysseus slept.

Nanna took charge over him

Eternal as all the gods.

Protecting him from the ravages

Of time.

As all around the temple, sand

And winds raged!

When Odysseus awoke refreshed

He found the wall around his room

Was drawn away

His clothes were strange,

His sandals replaced by

Combat boots.

His blouse bore a name

Odysseus, and on the other side,

U.S. Army

On his collar was a rank insignia

He did not know

The goddess had changed his appearance,

But left his mind unclouded.

Stumbling out of the Temple

He looked out at a land

Changed by time.

Large birds, made of metal

Flew to and fro,

Landing on a long strip nearby.

Metal giants made of what must be

Hardened bronze

Kicked up dust along the Desert below

Down the windswept steps he ran,

Toward these magical things

Suddenly he heard a man shout

In a language, he should not have known

"Who goes there! Identify yourself!"

Some distance away he saw a group

Dressed like him in kind

Advancing towards him,

Pointing strange spears at him.

"What unit are you with?

Hold there!"

The soldiers closed the distance

Seeing he was wearing the uniform

Of a Captain, they lowered their weapons.

"Sir', they called out

"What are you doing so far from the base?

We can give you a lift back.

What unit are you with?"

With the goddess's inspiration on his lips

He answered

"I am Capitan Odysseus, from Ithaca

77th Infantry Division."

He glanced at his shoulder and saw a cloth patch

Bearing the image of the Goddess Libertas

Holding high with one hand a torch of light

In the other bearing an old tome.

Feeling the inspiration draining from him

He asked,

"What war is this? What Army to we clearly hail from?

What in the name of the gods are we doing here?"

The soldiers looked confused, and said among themselves,

"He must be a heat casualty!"

Taking him with them, onto the back of a metal monster

They sped him back to their camp.

Passing the gate, Odysseus caught in his sight

A flag.

Blowing in dust and wind

It had stripes pure as snow

Stripes red as blood

And stars in a blue field

Of the divines.

From across the back of that metal monster

A soldier yelled to Odysseus

"Welcome to the suck, Sir!"

Odysseus collapsed from exhaustion and shock.

He was in Iraq.

Northward to Desolation

Odysseus rode inside a metal monster

Northward to besiege a city

The wind blew hard around the vehicle

Sand seemed to seep in everywhere

By now our Captain had been

In this new army six months

Learning what the goddess

Had not been revealed to him.

You had to keep your eyes on the road

Massive explosions like the thunderbolts of Zeus

Could arise without warning

Burning vehicles and men alike

He had seen three of those a week

Three times the thunderbolts had met their mark

Burning five of his men alive in the belly

Of that metal monster

Screaming in agony

Calling for their mothers

The Captain had tried to save them

But the flames burned hot

Forcing him away.

Blood and bone metal littered the pavement

While villagers screamed Allahu Akbar!

His anger at them grew with each passing day

His indifference to their plight festered

Like a puss-filled sore

As the cherry of his cigarette lit the night

The call to prayer sounded in the distance.

The City of Mosques

They encircled the city

All roads were closed off

Terrible catapults spit fire at the town in the distance

Those large metal rocks the catapults threw

Contained thunderbolts

Odysseus knew

Death would fall with them

On both the innocent and the guilty.

He had seen the enemy use them as well

Raining terror down upon his men as the slept

Or ate, or simply enjoyed some time off

Between patrols.

It rained metal in this strange land

No seer of sage cloud forecast that storm.

The men's hands would shake at the thought of that terror

That could strike without warning or mercy

Now they would return that fire to the enemy

One hundredfold.

In this free-fire zone

Everyone was a target.

No one could leave

White flag or not

The army had cornered its quarry.

Libertas Frees the City

When our hero entered the city

With the rearguard

He found a desolate place

The resistance was down to small pockets

Burned bodies covered the streets

Unburied.

Strange white mist from the catapults

Had stolen the breath

From their lungs

Odysseus saw a child there

Lying face up

His face covered in vomit

Odysseus wept.

He turned to one of his men and asked

"What the fuck is this all for?"

The man answered,

"Fucked if I know, Sir."

That was I, That was me. I was just as lost as him.

Poor bastards, both of us.

Home to Ithaca

Odysseus climbed into the belly of a metal bird

Its wings roared with the fury of the gods.

He watched the ground grow farther

And farther away.

He would finally see his beloved Ithaca.

When he saw the outline of Athens from the plane

He nearly wept but watched in horror as the city appeared

Strange to his eyes.

Once great buildings lay in ruins

And metal monsters crawled upon the ground.

He was terrified when his bird flew on

To an unknown destination.

Odysseus flew on over a vast ocean

More lost than ever before

He feared the goddess had abandoned him

If she had ever existed at all.

The bird came to rest in a strange place

Of the hustle and bustle

Something called "Starbucks" was everywhere.

A woman with the "MWR" welcoming committee

Threw her arms around Odysseus and yelled

"Welcome home, soldier!"

Odysseus tensed every muscle in his body

He had not been embraced for what seemed like forever

It felt like ten thousand years since then

He felt lost.

This was not his home.

The Hero Drunk: Home at last
In the Army, all is in order. When you leave, all is chaos.

    Years had passed

    Since Odysseus had returned

"home"

      He sat on a street corner

drinking

    His mixed wine

      Passersby threw coins

at him

    Others hurled insults

He wished, without reservation

      That he had died in place of

his friends

      He screamed to nobody

    "What a wretched death I'm

doomed to die!"

A man came by one day.

                                      Who told him about a meeting

               He might give a try to.

                                      "No one has

suffered more than me!"

He told the man who shook his head.

                                         "One

day at a time, my friend."

He responded, so full of love.

                                       "Easy

does it brother."

Serenity Now

                    "In that small room"

          Many veterans gathered

                        Worn out old soldiers

        Like Odysseus himself.

                        He heard many stories

of loss

                At that Ithica VA hospital A.A.

meeting.

                        Odysseus was

homeless

                A wayfarer

                        But the VA put

him in

                A sober living facility

                        Soon his mantra

had changed

                From "No one has suffered more than

me."

                        To

                "Everyone has suffered in their

own way."

                    As he continued to go

                    To the meetings

                    Work the steps

                                He found a new God to

call upon

                                A new prayer to pray

                                Every day before he left

his room

                                He prayed,

"God

Grant me the Serenity

To accept the things I cannot change

The courage to change the things I can

And the Wisdom to know the difference

Amen."

End Notes

[i] Army Year Book Fort Knox Kentucky, 2006
[ii] Goddard, Dwight, A Buddhist Bible, Beacon Press: 1970
[iii] https://www.sciencedirect.com/science/article/pii/S026974911834243X?via%3Dihub
[iv] https://www.ncbi.nlm.nih.gov/pmc/articles/PMC3492088/
[v] https://www.iaea.org/topics/spent-fuel-management/depleted-uranium
[vi] https://www.youtube.com/watch?v=XKfuS6gfxPY&t=22s
[vii] https://www.washingtonpost.com/news/politics/wp/2018/03/20/15-years-after-it-began-the-death-toll-from-the-iraq-war-is-still-murky/

Made in the USA
Monee, IL
17 February 2020